The New

SPELL WELL

C000128358

Book 4

C J Ridout

Nelson

Contents

Thomas Nelson and Sons Ltd
Nelson House Mayfield Road
Walton-on-Thames Surrey KT12 5PL UK

© Thomas Nelson and Sons Ltd 1992
First published by Blackie & Son Ltd 1978

This edition published by Thomas Nelson and Sons Ltd 1993

I⊤P Thomas Nelson is an International
Thomson Publishing Company

I⊤P is used under licence

ISBN 0-17-424555-6
NPN 9 8 7

1	2	3
piece	regular	though
field	popular	although
pierce	circular	together
fierce	singular	altogether

4	5	6
pleasant	begin	hollow
treasure	began	follow
measure	begun	swallow
pheasant	beginning	shallow

7	8	9
almost	edge	feather
always	hedge	leather
alone	wedge	heather
also	ledge	weather

10	11	12
excuse	phase	orphan
excite	phrase	nephew
except	photograph	prophet
excellent	telephone	alphabet

Hijacked!

aeroplane
stewardess
announcement
destination
passengers
captain
crew
navigator
flight deck
customs
cabin
galley
sandwiches
coffee
lemonade
gangway
baggage
hold
weapon
revolver
bomb

police
official
runway
grenade

reclining
flashing
excited
desperate
happy
joyful
pleasant
smooth
terrified
worried
thankful
masked
frightened
screaming
revving
anxious

yelled
refuelled
attacked
arrested
struggled
shouted
fainted
commanded
ordered
threatened
pointed
anticipated
taxied
banked
climbed
stumbled
embarked

unexpectedly
instantly
simultaneously

Phrases

fasten your seat belts
lowered the undercarriage
the departure lounge
cleared for take-off
an emergency landing
surrounded by police

customs check
threw off balance
a change of course
in radio contact
an armed guard
descended quickly

1	**2**	**3**
captain	angel	jewel
curtain	label	camel
certain	vessel	towel
Britain	parcel	model

4	**5**	**6**
forehead	habit	untidy
forenoon	limit	unwell
foremost	permit	unable
foresight	omit	unhappy

7	**8**	**9**
diamond	piano	column
diameter	violin	solemn
diagram	clarinet	hymn
diagonal	trumpet	condemn

10	**11**	**12**
retain	midday	long
entertain	midnight	length
sustain	midway	broad
certain	midsummer	breadth

Safari park

ranger
monkey
lion
tiger
zebra
cheetah
elephant
leopard
camel
giraffe
kangaroo
trees
restaurant
direction
vehicle
land rover
precautions
captivity
excitement
hide
camouflage
enclosure

freedom
pride
herd
animals

artificial
natural
favourite
friendly
indifferent
waving
exciting
anxious
loping
graceful
agile
surrounding
frightened
interested
watchful
magnificent
carnivorous

herbivorous
curious
inconspicuous
ferocious
angry
fierce
dangerous
hollow

supervised
retreated
reached
climbed
rode
snarled
roared
yawned

greedily
hungrily
warily
sleepily

Phrases
one-way traffic
free to roam
grabbed the wipers
seized the aerial
a haughty expression

clambered over the car
chunks of raw meat
high perimeter fence
"Keep windows closed"
lying sunning himself

7

1	2	3
vary	scent	general
varied	scene	generally
variety	scenery	special
various	science	specially

4	5	6
pound	cruel	respect
round	cruelty	expect
found	fuel	inspect
sound	duel	insect

7	8	9
till	exit	upper
until	extra	lower
skill	explain	inner
skilful	experience	outer

10	11	12
education	use	doubt
information	uses	doubtful
dictation	useful	debt
temptation	using	debtor

Dial 999 for police!

burglar
robber
crime
criminal
jeweller
jewellery
sapphire
emerald
silver
pendant
bracelet
watch
digital clock
gang
police siren
handcuffs
detective
proprietor
telephone
alley
lamplight

radio
message
description
safe
vault
combination
dynamite

dangerous
skilful
audacious
suspicious
cunning
careful
strident
quiet
precious
valuable
expensive
dishonest
wily

escaped
avoided
exploded
witnessed
shattered
planned
pursued
chased
caught
arrested
charged
grabbed
hid

boldly
frantically
bravely
recklessly
carefully
immediately
ruthlessly

Phrases

a getaway car
a deserted roadway
the scream of tyres
a fleeting shadow
a blue, flashing light
a muffled explosion

sparkling jewels
a revving engine
priceless diamonds
caught red-handed
a dazzling spotlight
brought to justice

1	**2**	**3**
correct	chief	behave
correction	mischief	behaviour
direct	handkerchief	save
direction	neckerchief	saviour

4	**5**	**6**
agree	add	state
agreed	subtract	estate
agreement	multiply	cultivate
agreeable	divide	decorate

7	**8**	**9**
avenue	first	colour
street	last	harbour
crescent	former	labour
road	latter	humour

10	**11**	**12**
fast	forgot	furnish
fasten	forgotten	furnished
haste	forget	furnishing
hasten	forgetting	furniture

The swimming pool

attendant
instructor
lesson
floats
shower
cafeteria
length
breadth
competitors
gala
butterfly
style
events
armbands
final
admission
spectator
gallery
bubbles
chlorine
towel
diving board
entrance

depth
locker
advice
shouts
exit

spluttering
shallow
deep
shivering
sensible
daring
tiled
rippling
sparkling
tiring
proud
busy
crowded
graceful
powerful
modern
watchful

cautious
helpful
prudent
laughing
magnificent
screeching
successful

enticed
persuaded
encouraged
ventured
dived
climbed
somersaulted
submerged
undressed
observed
splashed
crawled
clambered

reluctantly

Phrases
the breaststroke
a relay race
shrieks of delight
bobbing about

surged forward
a stylish swimmer
becoming more confident
a beautiful dive

11

1	**2**	**3**
weigh	number	lemonade
weighed	timber	squash
weight	member	cocoa
freight	remember	coffee

4	**5**	**6**
write	unit	cardboard
writing	union	maybe
written	unite	newspaper
wrote	unison	notebook

7	**8**	**9**
image	bless	fence
imagine	distress	reference
imagination	confess	sentence
imaginary	success	occurrence

10	**11**	**12**
windmill	ski	honour
teapot	skied	honest
seaport	skis	honesty
fireplace	skiing	honourable

Into battle

knight
armour
chain-mail
sword
spear
shield
visor
helmet
gauntlet
combat
tournament
contest
opponent
arena
victor
renown
spur
tent
joust
saddle

rein
exploits
prowess
charger
forfeit
pennant
plume
crusade

famous
handsome
pierce
distinguished
doughty
victorious
courteous
chivalrous
heraldic
weighty
honourable

successful
heroic
skilful

galloped
dismounted
fought
thrust
parried
tilted
protected
wounded
captured
pierced
penetrated
challenged
competed
vanquished
overcame
emblazoned

Phrases
fatally wounded
tumult of battle
in bygone days
a glancing blow
fought like a lion
of noble birth
skilled armourer

a haughty knight
glistened in the sunlight
a coal-black charger
the clash of steel
thundering hooves
hand-to-hand fight
splendid swordsman

1	**2**	**3**
err	listen	cushion
error	listener	fashion
erratic	listening	region
errand	listened	religion

4	**5**	**6**
succeed	addition	approach
exceed	subtraction	oath
proceed	multiplication	throat
procession	division	poach

7	**8**	**9**
bury	correct	people
buried	correction	needle
busy	direct	sprinkle
business	direction	trouble

10	**11**	**12**
electric	dismal	ease
electrical	discuss	easier
electrician	dismiss	easy
electricity	distress	easily

A visit to the park

swings
chute
roundabouts
bandstand
conservatory
terrace
lawn
shrubbery
attendant
gardener
kiosk
aquarium
aviary
rockery
arbour
trellis
fragrance
perfume
shelter
pond

toilets
fountain
sundial
statue
dovecot
leisure
ducks
geese
gosling
peacock
swan
cygnet
deer
green-house
annual
perennial
advantage
cluster

fragrant

magnificent
picturesque
abundant
exquisite
rustic
quaint
bright
brilliant

extend
flourish
possess
wander
mingle
adorn
waft
provide

beyond
orderly

Phrases
spacious lawns
herbaceous borders
tennis courts
to please the eye
a riot of colour
chattering squirrels
of every hue

a tour of inspection
a little, shady nook
growing in profusion
laughing children
fragrant honeysuckle
twittering birds
long, light evenings

1	**2**	**3**
orchestra	penknife	serial
stomach	streamline	material
chemist	outdoors	aerial
mechanic	armchair	imperial

4	**5**	**6**
moment	built	route
second	quilt	wound
minute	guilt	youth
hour	guilty	group

7	**8**	**9**
wreck	inform	object
wrist	reform	subject
wriggle	deform	direct
wrong	uniform	protect

10	**11**	**12**
wage	draught	information
courage	enough	population
passage	quay	association
language	queue	appreciation

A foggy day

autumn
November
weather
gloom
atmosphere
phantom
crevice
temperature
caution
accident
disaster
safety
distance
traffic
hindrance
smog
visibility
lights
pavement

swirling
clinging
sudden
smoky
murky
dense
considerable
extraordinary
impossible
dangerous
frequent
usual
cautious
several
common

loom
extend
surround

occur
hinder
delay
cease
disappear
envelop
penetrate
endanger
prevent
recognize
travel
obscure
pierce
depress

completely
especially
extremely
faintly

Phrases

impenetrable gloom
muffled tread
to hurry homewards
dark and dismal
a vague outline
at a snail's pace
barely visible
moaning foghorns

the lamps' pale beams
to lose one's way
every nook and cranny
with considerable
    difficulty
a blanket of mist
no sense of direction
ghostly figures

1	**2**	**3**
dizzy	wake	content
puzzle	woke	consent
dazzle	awaken	prevent
drizzle	awakening	eventful

4	**5**	**6**
rice	observe	mean
spice	reserve	meaning
device	preserve	means
advice	deserve	meant

7	**8**	**9**
teacher	travel	gain
trainer	traveller	regain
gardener	travelling	again
announcer	travelled	against

10	**11**	**12**
reindeer	home	shout
cupboard	abroad	doubt
green-house	native	bough
night-dress	foreign	plough

U.F.O !

shape
horizon
beam
orbit
Earth
planet
space
arc
cylinder
outline
theory
curiosity
photograph
reporter
newspaper
suspicious
speculation
disbelief
precaution
description
congratulations

unintelligible
observant
indistinct
mysterious
supernatural
metallic
spherical
whistling
spinning
distant
shimmering
glowing
curious
wary
watchful

landed
hovered
descended
narrated
searched

contacted
enquired
approached
informed
observed
deceived
lured
paused
peered

disbelievingly
unexpectedly
automatically
apparently
hesitantly
cautiously
quickly
suddenly
suspiciously
visibly
behind

Phrases

unidentified flying object
eye-witness account
previous sightings
contact the authorities
became a celebrity
newspaper report

banner headlines
flattened grass
knowing looks
clearly visible
a television interview
beyond doubt

1	**2**	**3**
eager	charge	dance
weave	change	prance
defeat	orchard	fancy
preach	purchase	mercy

4	**5**	**6**
reason	noble	rare
season	eagle	dare
feature	kindle	scare
creature	castle	square

7	**8**	**9**
due	guess	elect
glue	guessed	neglect
argue	guessing	select
rescue	guerrilla	erect

10	**11**	**12**
real	noun	overcoat
really	adjective	Iceland
peal	verb	teaspoon
appeal	adverb	bookcase

A walk by moonlight

moonbeam
crescent
stars
forest
copse
thicket
village
hamlet
thatch
roofs
surface
crystal
expanse
glade
destination
experience
silence
reflection
building
landscape

clear
tranquil
peaceful
silvery
stately
curious
glistening
eerie
ghostly
mysterious
gliding
sudden
startling
familiar
circular
lunar
different
unusual
unreal
colourless

stroll
wander
approach
advance
border
assume
appear
disappear
adorn
twinkle
retrace
frame
explore
illuminate

quietly
calmly
silently
thoughtfully
suddenly

Phrases

ghostly silhouettes
eerie silence
silver-tipped petals
moonlit world
the sleeping village
racing clouds
shimmering water

a gossamer web
shaft of moonlight
a cloud's silver lining
whisper of the breeze
calm and cloudless
startling hoot of an owl
yellow harvest moon

21

1	**2**	**3**
knight	figure	damage
kneel	endure	package
known	scripture	voyage
unknown	assure	advantage

4	**5**	**6**
write	due	inquire
wring	flue	enquire
wreath	value	enquiry
wrap	statue	require

7	**8**	**9**
metal	refer	town
total	reference	country
mental	confer	urban
pedal	conference	rural

10	**11**	**12**
terror	random	horror
terrible	seldom	horrible
terrified	stardom	horrified
terrifying	kingdom	horrifying

Forest fire

plantation
spruce
larch
warden
ranger
roadway
cloud
tongue
spark
smoke
flame
blaze
heat
inferno
furnace
dynamite
ashes
embers
emergency
apparatus
beaters

firemen
telephone
animals
bulldozer
reinforcements
boughs
branches

anxious
devouring
suffocating
disastrous
auxiliary
wispy
dense
crackling
bare
stark
stifling
ghostly
smouldering

charred
leaping
deafening
terrifying
exhausted
blistered
unrecognizable

ignited
scorched
contained
evacuated
felled
altered
investigated
prevented
answered
summoned
threatened
engulfed
spread

Phrases

a look-out tower
blackened with soot
showered with sparks
withdrew to safety
rays of the sun
a path of destruction

fanned by the wind
spread like wildfire
a careless act
toppled in flames
a broken bottle
the glowing embers

1	**2**	**3**
exist	recall	several
exhaust	result	general
expert	remind	gradual
example	revenge	animal

4	**5**	**6**
exact	gracious	discuss
attract	precious	disgust
subtract	delicious	disgrace
extract	anxious	disgraceful

7	**8**	**9**
remove	royal	conduct
remark	loyal	conductor
reduce	spiral	convict
resume	local	conviction

10	**11**	**12**
sufficient	amuse	medal
insufficient	amusement	capital
efficient	engage	external
inefficient	engagement	rascal

A day in a big city

road
avenue
terrace
crescent
architecture
museum
theatre
church
cathedral
spire
dome
cinema
art gallery
hotel
restaurant
office block
residence
warehouse
store

monument
statue
arches
pillars
traffic
taxi
bicycle
business
centre
fountain
citizen
people
policeman
warden
tourists
shoppers
jeweller's
clothes
furniture

crowded
historical
inspiring
incessant
residential

travel
congregate
assemble
view
explore
reside
succeed
achieve
remain
linger
admire
wonder
examine

Phrases
places of interest
the busy streets
board a bus
stately, old buildings
the heart of the city
pedestrian precinct
thronging the pavements
the latest fashions

roar of the traffic
a panoramic view
shop-window display
relics of the past
a stream of commuters
a pelican crossing
patrolling traffic
wardens

1	**2**	**3**
confess	fetch	timetable
condition	stretch	headache
conceal	snatch	football
confuse	kitchen	staircase

4	**5**	**6**
school	conspire	pie
scholar	control	sandwich
scheme	consider	biscuit
chemist	contain	sponge

7	**8**	**9**
embarrass	separate	medicine
embarrassed	separated	poison
embarrassment	separating	spoonful
embarrassing	separation	hygiene

10	**11**	**12**
gym	woollen	secret
gymnasium	committee	secretary
gymnast	commission	sign
gymnastics	assassination	signature

Diving for treasure

bubbles
cylinder
oxygen
depths
torch
galleon
bullion
gold
coins
chest
wreck
porthole
skeleton
vessel
cannon
flippers
cask
seaweed
fortune
secret

direction
jellyfish
lobster
crab
barnacles
limpets
cave

Spanish
wrecked
sunken
broken
camouflaged
concealed
hidden
nervous
impossible
delighted
thrilling
wonderful

floated
searched
peered
dragged
dived
gathered
noticed
occupied
stumbled
followed

dangerously
successfully
gradually
desperately
painfully
worriedly
suspiciously
cautiously
mysteriously

Phrases
tugged the life-line
circling sharks
magic, underwater world
an exciting discovery
an undiscovered hulk
a necessary precaution
permission to investigate

twenty fathoms down
shoals of fish
secrets of the deep
gliding silently past
transparent shrimps
Neptune's kingdom
broke the surface

1	**2**	**3**
suitable	important	quality
valuable	abundant	quantity
constable	pleasant	quarrel
vegetable	attendant	qualify

4	**5**	**6**
bedroom	diction	behave
bathroom	friction	because
handsome	satisfaction	beneath
lamplight	destruction	betray

7	**8**	**9**
cheerful	comfort	irritate
beautiful	comfortable	irritation
delightful	company	irrigate
wonderful	companion	irrigation

10	**11**	**12**
admit	occur	sentence
admission	occurrence	reference
permit	recur	existence
permission	recurrence	commence

28

The fête

marquee
table
hoop-la
competition
champion
prize
price
entrance
ornaments
donkey
shower
umbrella
clamour
lemonade
squash
ice-cream
toffee apples
coconut
baking
vegetables
refreshments
sandwiches

candy
tablet
fruit
bottle
afternoon
blooms
scent
perfume
bouquets
crowd

enjoyable
beautiful
grassy
exhausting
tempting
attractive
sultry
excited
eager
successful
wooden

juicy
cheerful
busy
miniature
magnificent
proud
light-hearted
noisy
skilful
enjoyable

displayed
won
judged
mingled
awarded
attended
wandered
strolled
bought
tasted
munched

Phrases
a giant marrow
took careful aim
for charity
cloudless sky
white elephant stall

admission free
a riot of colour
flags of all nations
"Roll up, roll up"
fortune-teller's tent

29

Points of the compass

north	south	east	west
northern	southern	eastern	western
northerly	southerly	easterly	westerly

Articles of clothing

trousers	blouse	jacket
blazer	overcoat	raincoat
cardigan	jersey	anorak
gloves	slippers	pyjamas

Fish

herring	mackerel	plaice
salmon	trout	cod

Meat

beef	mutton	pork
venison	lamb	veal

Poultry and game

chicken	turkey	goose
pheasant	duck	partridge

Parts of the body

heart	heel	mouth
throat	shoulder	fingers
ankle	tongue	ear
wrist	thigh	chest
limb	knee	head
thumb	nose	elbow
stomach	forehead	spine

Life in the Middle Ages

castle
drawbridge
portcullis
moat
soldier
knight
armour
tournament
archery
traveller
hospitality
monastery
monk
friar
pedlar
peasant
banquet
trencher
ale

crossbow
battlements
jester
siege
fair
pilgrimage
shrine
guild
apprentice
village
yeomen
deer
venison
oxen
maypole
merchant
jollity
stocks
pillory

woollen
wooden
unpleasant
hospitable
harsh
colourful
ornamental
massive

wrestle
shoot
practise
hunt
labour
preach
punish
joust
trade
gather

Phrases

in Merrie England
bands of pilgrims
a travelling fair
the dreaded plague
to offer hospitality
wattle and daub
common pasture
rich embroidery

lord of the manor
thick castle walls
a line of pack-horses
a strolling player
fallow fields
narrow, filthy streets
a wandering minstrel
a hooded falcon

Capital cities

London	Paris	Copenhagen
Brussels	Washington	Vienna
Moscow	Bonn	Berlin
Lisbon	Reykjavik	Madrid
Ottawa	Stockholm	Canberra
Wellington	Athens	Belgrade
Warsaw	Rome	Tokyo

Famous rivers

Rhine	Rhone	Ganges
Mississippi	Missouri	Seine
Amazon	Danube	Nile

Books and publications

atlas	dictionary	directory
magazine	catalogue	timetable
diary	map	newspaper
bible	novel	manual

Buildings

cathedral	church	theatre
museum	cottage	cinema
prison	barracks	factory
school	castle	warehouse

Wild animals

gorilla	tiger	giraffe
elephant	leopard	gnu
orang-utan	kangaroo	zebra
cheetah	chimpanzee	rhinoceros

Life as a cowboy

America
prairie
cattle
herd
steer
mustang
stallion
piebald
corral
stampede
lasso
foreman
revolver
holster
boundary
precaution
bunkhouse
neckerchief
railroad
rustler

chaps
stetson
stirrup
saddle
reins
cactus

strenuous
thrilling
sturdy
skilful
agile
gallant
vast
adventurous
speedy
healthy
valuable
sunburnt
desperate

hazardous
daring

described
mounted
occurred
cantered
galloped
eluded
branded
enclosed
pastured
thrown
caught
considered
achieved
employed
endured
strayed
guided

Phrases

rolling prairies
spurred his horse
an abrupt stop
maddened cattle
a rough trail
hobbled the horses
covered wagons

annual round-up
rode like the wind
endured hardships
lasso the steers
a consignment of beef
the horse's flanks
cast a shoe

Metals

copper	iron	steel	chromium
zinc	silver	gold	lead
tin	platinum	nickel	aluminium

alloy—a mixture of metals

Woods

oak	walnut	spruce	cedar
pine	mahogany	teak	ebony
elm	bamboo	balsa	ash

veneer—a thin leaf of decorative wood
ply—thin layers of wood glued together

Shopping list

butter	margarine	biscuits
currants	raisins	detergent
spaghetti	yoghurt	cheese
toothpaste	marmalade	barley

National emblems

England—rose   Wales—daffodil and leek
Scotland—thistle   Ireland—shamrock

Money

Britain	100 pence = one pound
France	100 centimes = one franc
United States	100 cents = one dollar

Greece—drachma   Russia—rouble
Spain—peseta   Japan—yen
Germany—mark   Italy—lira

A thunderstorm

thunderbolt
thunderclap
peal
warning
interval
lightning
conductor
spire
torrent
deluge
drizzle
electricity
charge
succession
vibration
thrill
turmoil
protection
shelter
distance

forked
noisy
zigzag
sudden
overcast
sultry
leaden
vivid
distant
incessant
severe
violent
fierce
frequent
bedraggled
deserted
suffocating

resound
echo

soak
drench
occur
attract
appear
accompany
dazzle
teem
illuminate
threaten
cease
abate
terrify
destroy
strike

hurriedly
immediately
continuously
loudly

Phrases

distant thunder
blinding flash
paralysed with fear
mass of black clouds
an ill-fated tree
not a leaf rustled
a few moments' interval

to take cover
almost deafened
across the heavens
frightened cattle
flooded roads
without warning
peace reigned

Some ways of forming plurals

1   Words ending in y :

| key | keys | chimney | chimneys |
| tray | trays | donkey | donkeys |

When y is preceded by a vowel—add –s.

ruby	rubies	factory	factories
memory	memories	difficulty	difficulties
lady	ladies	library	libraries
injury	injuries	robbery	robberies

When y is preceded by a consonant—change –y into –i and add –es.

2   Words ending in o :

solo	solos	potato	potatoes
folio	folios	tomato	tomatoes
Eskimo	Eskimos	hero	heroes
piano	pianos	negro	negroes

Some add –s.   Some add –es.

3   Add en :

| ox | oxen |

Add ren :

| child | children |

4   Change vowel sound :

man	men	woman	women
mouse	mice	foot	feet
tooth	teeth	goose	geese

5   Words which stay the same :

| sheep | salmon | fish | deer |
| cod | herring | trout | you |

The story of coal

forest
vegetation
mosses
ferns
jungle
creatures
miner
helmet
machinery
wagon
safety
precaution
safety lamp
gas
pit-head
shaft
gallery
ventilation
electricity
Yorkshire
fuel
discomfort

explosive
apparatus
equipment
conditions
inspector
difficulty

primeval
gigantic
luxuriant
swampy
abundant
dense
enormous
extensive
necessary
unhealthy
damp
mechanical
dirty
courageous
heavy

laborious
dangerous
reliable
uncomfortable

compress
bury
descend
transport
extract
evacuate
detonate
ignite
support
control
explode
haul
sift
convey
grade
crawl
ascend

Phrases
open-cast mining
fossil remains
carboniferous rocks
creaking pit-props
black diamonds

a rich seam
inferior quality
as black as night
poisonous gases
superior grade

Some more ways of forming plurals

6 Words borrowed from other languages :

radius	radii	phenomenon	phenomena
syllabus	syllabuses	cumulus	cumuli
stratum	strata	basis	bases
axis	axes	maximum	maxima
minimum	minima	memorandum	memoranda
oasis	oases	curriculum	curricula

7 Words used in plural only :

bellows	pincers	pliers	scissors
shears	dividers	tongs	trousers
jeans	measles	pyjamas	tweezers

8 Compound words :

court martial	courts martial
father-in-law	fathers-in-law
passer-by	passers-by
coat-of-mail	coats-of-mail
man-of-war	men-of-war
lady-in-waiting	ladies-in-waiting
brother-in-law	brothers-in-law
sister-in-law	sisters-in-law
Member of Parliament	Members of Parliament

Note :

teaspoonful	teaspoonfuls
dessertspoonful	dessertspoonfuls
tablespoonful	tablespoonfuls

The cinema

placard
advertisement
performance
programme
matinee
queue
admission
ticket
confectionery
chocolates
cartoon
detective
western
gangster
cowboy
screen
stalls
balcony
actor
actress

hero
heroine
usherette
audience
comedian
antics
scene
interval
curtain
exit
cafe

numerous
comfortable
spectacular
educational
historical
pathetic
humorous
favourite

serious
famous
fabulous
amusing
exciting
hilarious
mysterious

advertise
enthral
appeal
imagine
produce
extinguish
project
imagine

usually
especially
recently

Phrases

dimly lit auditorium
ideal afternoon pastime
interest and amusement
favourite film star
a tense moment
took the leading part
forthcoming attractions

a double feature
science fiction
vary in price
supporting film
theme tune
to leave with regret
sit spell-bound

Books

Preface—introductory remarks to a book.
Often tells you why a book has been written.

Contents—list of headings telling you what is in
the book.

Index—table of references in alphabetical order.
Helps you to find a specific piece of information
quickly.

Alphabetical order

In books of reference such as dictionaries and
encyclopedias it is necessary to arrange words
in such an order that they can be easily found.
The easiest method is to place words in alphabetical order.

eagle   giant   school   unicorn   zero
Look at the order of the first letters.

label   leisure   license   longitude
When the first letters are the same, look at the
order of the second letters.

dahlia   daily   dainty   dairy   daisy
When the first two letters are the same, look at
the order of the third letters, and so on.

Arrange the listed words on pages 33, 35, & 37
in alphabetical order.

My favourite book

novel
novelist
author
writer
hero
heroine
villain
character
fiction
non-fiction
episode
series
volume
chapter
paragraph
climax
exploit
plot
setting
adventure
exploration

legend
fable
travel
poetry
information
encyclopedia
excitement
enjoyment
mystery
incident

interesting
thrilling
unusual
famous
descriptive
factual
historical
realistic
humorous
instructive

educational
attractive
expensive

treasure
possess
collect
absorb
enjoy
concentrate
study
illustrate
delight
discover

avidly
thoroughly
completely
greatly
carefully
dearly

Phrases

thrilling adventure
a well-known classic
buried in a book
an absorbing story
living in the past
a long, winter evening

dog-eared and worn
a sigh of relief
a welcome gift
well read and loved
beautifully bound
a tale to remember

Words which can be confused—I

Check the meaning of each word in your dictionary. Then write the word in a sentence.

Round 1

bare	bough	dew	fare
feat	heel	quay	pail
peal	plane	pore	prey

Round 2

reed	wring	site	soar
sow	bury	chord	coarse
grate	groan	hire	whole

Round 3

knight	pause	plaice	plumb
source	stake	stare	steel
waist	aloud	angle	assent

Round 4

borough	ceiling	cellar	cheque
council	currant	gaol	guest
holy	aisle	lesson	lightning
tale	there	sail	altar

Round 5

practice	principal	prophet	stationery
weather	yolk	bean	through
piece	beech	flour	hare
gambol	deer	muscle	pane

A storm at sea

ocean
breakers
surf
spray
spume
shingle
squall
gale
thunder
rocket
flare
rescue
lifeboat
lighthouse
fury
despair
sailor
hero
coastguard

turbulent
grey
greedy
relentless
angry
wrathful
tremendous
powerful
courageous
wintry
tragic
treacherous
warning
raging
quiet
tranquil
aloft
aboard
terrifying

pound
crash
pitch
whistle
lash
hurl
fight
roar
capsize
deafen
wreck
shriek
resist
subside
triumph
abate
battle
engulf
swallow

Phrases

flashes of lightning
the gallant vessel
a sudden squall
tossed like a cork
in sore distress
the pitiless sea
with tremendous force
ominous clouds

lull in the storm
treacherous rocks
shriek of the wind
a raging tempest
a peal of thunder
revealed in flashes
mountainous waves
sheets of rain

Masculine and feminine (male and female)

bachelor	spinster	widower	widow
stallion	mare	heir	heiress
nephew	niece	uncle	aunt
emperor	empress	billy-goat	nanny-goat
fox	vixen	master	mistress

Pair the masculine and feminine words in the following lists.
Use your dictionary where necessary.

Round 6

cow	sow	princess	ram
nun	bride	sir	actress
bridegroom	lady	ewe	duck
boar	bull	actor	madam
lord	monk	drake	prince

Round 7

wizard	buck	marquis	executrix
filly	countess	gander	stag
earl	lion	negro	marchioness
doe	witch	hind	negress
lioness	colt	executor	goose

Round 8

duke	sultana	god	hero
mayor	bullock	landlord	prophet
authoress	duchess	heroine	peahen
sultan	author	prophetess	landlady
heifer	mayoress	peacock	goddess

An autobiography

appearance
complexion
address
nationality
British
English
Welsh
Scottish
Irish
West Indian
Pakistani
friends
teacher
school
height
weight
hobby
sport
family
parents
brother
sister
nephew

relations
niece
twins
cousin
aunt
uncle
birthday
grandfather
grandmother
measles
mumps
television
pocket money
collection
playground
bicycle
ambition

auburn
brunette
polite
industrious
obedient

athletic
artistic
musical
miserable
strict
stern
indifferent
eventful
younger
eldest
keen
intelligent

persuade
prefer
resemble
dislike
enjoy
visit

especially
recently
usually

Phrases

the happiest time
the worst experience
my first memory
my pet aversion

best subject at school
my closest friend
my choice of book
a special treat

45

The apostrophe

Study these phrases :
1   the boy's house   the lady's hair
    the woman's clothes   the child's book
2   the boys' house   the ladies' hair
    the women's clothes   the children's book

Note :
1   When one thing possesses, we add 's.
2   When two or more possess, and the plural ends in –s, we simply add '.
If the plural does not end in –s, we add 's.

Rule—for possession we always add 's except for plural words ending in –s where we simply add '.

Round 9
Complete the following. The first one has been done for you.

the coat of the girl   the girl's coat
the tail of the dog   the cry of the gulls
the howl of the wind   the rays of the sun
the hats of the men   the fleece of the sheep
the wonders of Nature   the cover of the book

At the docks

estuary
vessel
quay
wharf
engine
engineer
machinery
crane
consignment
warehouse
gangway
siren
cable
hawser
bollard
docker
customs
buoy
radar
scanner

stevedore
chain
depot
pilot
tanker
container
office
truck
signal
lorry
official

international
refrigerated
enormous
foreign
huge
luxurious
heavy
skilful

mechanical
magnificent
thronging
principal
extensive
immense
powerful
continual

proceed
discharge
disembark
continue
import
export
permit
overhaul
inspect
direct
pile

Phrases

a forest of masts
throbbing engines
a gigantic liner
the busy tugs
unloading the crates
a ship's siren
in dry dock

flags of all nations
the Plimsoll line
cavernous holds
bustling with activity
the tang of the sea air
fenders creaking loudly
high in the water

Words which can be confused—II

Check the meaning of each word in your dictionary. Then write the word in a sentence.

Round 10

bear	bow	due	fair
feet	heal	key	pale
peel	plain	pour	pray

Round 11

read	ring	sight	sore
sew	berry	cord	course
great	grown	higher	hole

Round 12

night	paws	place	plum
sauce	steak	stair	steal
waste	allowed	angel	ascent

Round 13

burrow	sealing	seller	check
counsel	current	goal	guessed
wholly	isle	lessen	lightening
tail	their	sale	alter

Round 14

practise	principle	profit	stationary
whether	yoke	been	threw
peace	beach	flower	hair
gamble	dear	mussel	pain

A mountain climb

summit
peak
precipice
crag
scree
valley
ravine
gorge
torrent
waterfall
reservoir
moorlands
heather
turf
scenery
boulder
pylon
anorak
mountaineer

agile
active
energetic
difficult
marshy
perilous
dangerous
rushing
gushing
trickling
roaring
hazy
refreshing
weary
splendid
chilly
treacherous
cloudy
steep

magnificent
loose
strenuous
above
below
exhausting
exhilarating

ascend
glimpse
descend
scale
overcome
endure
accomplish
achieve
imperil
discern
endanger

Phrases

a narrow track
clinging mist
a competent guide
a strong breeze
dangerous descent
mountain tarn
a rocky outcrop
a sheer drop

trickling down
fertile valley
with great difficulty
feat of endurance
in the dim distance
precipitous path
awe-inspiring view
a miniature world

Letter writing

1   Address and date :
                        25 High Street
                        Newtown
                        West Midlands
                        WA4 3JT
                        7th March 1980

2   Greeting :
        Dear Mother   Dear Aunt Mary
        Dear Mr Smith   Dear Sir
        Dear Miss Jones   Dear Madam

3   Conclusion :
        Yours sincerely   Yours truly
        Yours faithfully   With love

4   Addressing an envelope :
                        C. E. Smith, Esq.
                        38 Diptree Street
                        Maidenport
                        Devon
                        AB2 0RB

Names

Full name   Charles Edward Stuart
Forenames (Christian names)   Charles Edward
Surname   Stuart
Initials   C. E. S.

Letter to a pen friend describing Christmas

decorations
preparations
fairylights
presents
parcels
cards
carols
bustle
hustle
shopping
surprise
secret
mistletoe
holly
berries
turkey
plum-pudding
mince-pies
paper hats
crackers
novelties

balloons
suspense
party
pantomime
theatre
circus
holiday
church
reindeer
sleigh
chimney
invitation
excitement
laughter
postman
deliveries

special
magnificent
attractive
funny

busy
numb
frozen
brilliant
scarlet
spectacular
interesting
white
overcast

buy
skate
ski
dazzle
discover
appeal
amuse
hide
address
entertain
purchase

Phrases

a nativity scene
colourful paper chains
magic of Christmas Eve
family reunions
"Just what I wanted!"
"A merry Christmas"

gay wrapping-paper
a mantle of snow
last-minute rush
season of goodwill
winter sports
lie awake all night

Opposites—using a different word

ancient	modern	interesting	dull
arrival	departure	junior	senior
cruel	kind	hope	despair
guilty	innocent	praise	blame

Pair the opposites in the following lists. Use your dictionary where necessary.

Round 15

failure	agile	knowledge	truth
asleep	grief	noisy	ignorance
joy	clever	slow	silent
stupid	awake	deliberate	rapid
clumsy	success	falsehood	accidental

Round 16

wise	attack	courage	exit
harmony	hurry	miserly	rough
loiter	discord	smooth	generous
fertile	foolish	entrance	public
defend	barren	private	cowardice

Round 17

pain	poverty	graceful	young
tough	pride	capture	calm
humility	expand	stormy	valuable
folly	pleasure	danger	awkward
contract	wisdom	old	release
wealth	tender	worthless	safety

A woodland walk

glade
dell
copse
chorus
melody
perfume
scent
rivulet
brook
eddy
reflection
current
course
source
burrow
trunk
bough
beech-mast
fir-cones
undergrowth

silence
anemone
bluebell
violet
bramble
nature
breeze

leafy
decayed
sturdy
rugged
lofty
stunted
gnarled
towering
ancient
mossy
erect
tuneful

sighing
gentle
many
furry
gloomy
shady
swaying
tall

wander
amble
whisper
hesitate
scamper
retreat
hurry
rustle
shiver
babble
spread

Phrases

stately elm tree
a gnarled oak
tender green leaves
monarch of the forest
the cuckoo's call
a gurgling stream
cawing rooks

slender silver birch
tap of a woodpecker
carpet of leaves
fallen branch
stillness of evening
cooing doves
swarms of midges

Opposites—using a prefix

sense	nonsense	loyal	disloyal
perfect	imperfect	direct	indirect
regular	irregular	noble	ignoble
just	unjust	legal	illegal

Pair the opposites.
Round 13

pure	unskilful	visible	correct
skilful	please	incorrect	disobey
displease	impure	grateful	ungrateful
impossible	possible	obey	invisible

Round 14

healthy	misuse	worthy	discomfort
impolite	distrust	unconscious	misfortune
faithful	behave	comfort	unhappy
use	unhealthy	unselfish	conscious
misbehave	polite	fortune	unworthy
trust	unfaithful	happy	selfish

Opposites—changing the prefix

ascent	descent	increase	decrease
inside	outside	include	exclude

Pair the opposites.
Round 15

export	external	immigrate	encourage
emigrate	discourage	import	internal

Nessie, the Loch Ness monster

twilight
darkness
gloom
reflection
reptile
creature
description
reporter
apparition
depths
fathom
sightseer
ripples
waves
telescope
binoculars
jaws
texture
armour
nightmare
dream

imagination
reappearance
view
horizon
mountain

gigantic
colossal
undulating
frightening
terrifying
horrifying
unreal
inquisitive
solitary
scaly
underwater
brief
eerie
gloomy
prehistoric

submerged
narrated
described
claimed
reared
waited
revealed
snorted
covered
disappeared
vanished
observed
believed

patiently
repeatedly
excitedly
momentarily
rapidly
carefully
earnestly

Phrases
a local inhabitant
while out fishing
surveyed the landscape
stared in disbelief
bewildered expression
stood transfixed

tourist attraction
stark outline
last dinosaur
black silhouette
murky depths
broke the surface

Abbreviations

A.D.	(L. *anno Domini*) in the year of our Lord	B.A.	British Airways
		B.C.	Before Christ
		c/o	care of
a.m.	(L. *ante meridiem*) before noon	St	Saint
		RSVP	(Fr. *répondez, s'il vous plaît*) please reply
p.m.	(L. *post meridiem*) after noon		
		No.	(It. *numero*) number
BBC	British Broadcasting Corporation		
		Dr	Doctor
ITV	Independent Television	Mr	Mister
		Mrs	Mistress
		Esq.	Esquire
e.g.	(L. *exempli gratia*) for example	Rev.	Reverend
		p.	page
		pp.	pages
etc.	(L. *et cetera*) and the rest	i.e.	(L. *id est*) that is
H.M.I.	Her Majesty's Inspector	IOU	I owe you
		PS.	postscript
		lat.	latitude
O.H.M.S.	On Her Majesty's Service	long.	longitude
		M.P.	Member of Parliament
U.S.A.	United States of America	U.K.	United Kingdom
B.R.	British Rail	$	dollar

Homes

A palace is the home of a king or bishop.
A drey is the home of a squirrel.

Match the home with the owners.
Round 16

byre	earth	burrow	cell
foxes	form	prisoners	hives
hares	cows	bees	rabbits

Round 17

kennel	stable	garage	set
vicarage	hangar	lions	lodge
aircraft	clergymen	beavers	den
horses	dogs	badgers	cars

Noises made by animals

dogs	bark	geese	hiss

Match the animals with their sounds.
Round 18

bees	asses	sheep	caw
bray	birds	crows	bleat
chirrup	buzz	bellow	bulls

Round 19

wolves	turkeys	bears	bark
horses	grunt	cows	trumpet
gobble	howl	elephants	low
pigs	neigh	dogs	growl

Opposites—changing the suffix

merciful   merciless   careful   careless

Pair the opposites.
Round 20

useful	cheerful	joyful	pitiful
pitiless	joyless	cheerless	useless

Animal young

a young dog   puppy
a young bear or lion   cub

Match up each animal with its young. Use your dictionary to help you.
Round 21

a young swan	foal, colt, filly
a young bird	fawn
a young horse	cygnet
a young deer	grilse
a young salmon	fledgling or nestling

Round 22

a young seal	gosling
a young hare	lamb
a young duck	kitten
a young goose	eaglet
a young sheep	pup
a young cat	leveret
a young eagle	duckling

Professions

An astronomer studies the heavenly bodies.
A dentist looks after teeth.

Use your dictionary to find out what the following people do.

Round 23

optician	anaesthetist	pharmacist
surveyor	architect	chiropodist
composer	ambassador	vet

Round 24

sculptor	biographer	chaplain
auditor	librarian.	physician
surgeon	artist	accountant

Round 25

editor	dietician	registrar
solicitor	radiographer	musician
playwright	producer	barrister

Trades

A fishmonger sells fish.
A decorator paints the insides of houses.

Use your dictionary to find out what the following people do.

Round 26

glazier	stationer	draper	butcher
mechanic	plumber	florist	confectioner

Scientific instruments

A microscope magnifies tiny objects.

Use your dictionary to find out what the following instruments do.

Round 27

thermometer	plumb-line	magnet
barometer	microphone	theodolite

Round 28

stethoscope	telescope	computer
binoculars	camera	compass
telephone	metronome	anemometer

Collections

a pack of hounds
a bench of magistrates

Match the collective word with its member.

Round 29

board	directors	stars	galaxy
covey	partridges	gaggle	flock
grapes	bunch	sheep	geese

Round 30

people	herd	whales	lions
bees	gang	pride	team
thieves	hive	scouts	school
cattle	crowd	horses	troop

Government

Hereditary head of a nation	King or Queen
Elected head of a republic	President
Head of an empire	Emperor
Head of a government	Prime Minister
Minister of finance	Chancellor of Exchequer
Ministers who govern a country	Cabinet
Persons eminent in politics	Statesmen and stateswomen
Chief law-making council	Parliament
Representative of the Sovereign	Ambassador

The solar system

Planets:

Pluto	Neptune	Uranus	Saturn
Jupiter	Mars	Earth	Venus
Mercury			

The Earth spins round on its axis once in 24 hours.

The Moon takes about a month to go round the Earth.

The Earth takes $364\frac{1}{4}$ days to go round the Sun.

The Moon is a satellite of the Earth.

Man-made satellites transmit weather information.

Special places

A dentist treats his patients in a surgery.
A typist works in an office.

Find out what happens in the following places.
Round 31

distillery	Mint	dispensary	dairy
brewery	studio	seminary	chambers
tannery	mill	observatory	laboratory

Inhabitants of countries

People born in France are French.

Match up the inhabitants with their countries.
Round 32

Britain	Ireland	Australia	India
England	Wales	N. Zealand	Zambia
Scotland	Canada	Pakistan	Egypt
Indians	Egyptians	British	Irish
Zambians	Pakistanis	N. Zealanders	Canadians
Welsh	Australians	Scots	English

Round 33

Austria	Holland	Poland	Sweden
Belgium	Germany	China	Switzerland
Denmark	Norway	Spain	Japan
Chinese	Austrians	Norwegians	Swedes
Germans	Dutch	Danes	Poles
Japanese	Spaniards	Belgians	Swiss

Words you may find useful

Use your dictionary to find out what they mean.

apiary	aviary	aquarium
bovine	carnivorous	canine
distillery	eaves	eavesdropper
hatchery	solarium	nature reserve
octave	planetarium	sanctuary

Performances

one person	solo	two persons	duet
three persons	trio	four persons	quartet

Similes

as clear as crystal
as cool as a cucumber
as light as a feather
as stubborn as a mule
as keen as mustard

as proud as a peacock
as steady as a rock
as sober as a judge
as hard as nails
as dead as a doornail

Nautical terms

starboard	right-hand side (green light)
port	left-hand side (red light)
prow or stem	the fore part of a ship
stern	the hind part of a ship
ebb	tide going out
flow	tide coming in
companionway	stairs
galley	kitchen

Inventions and discoveries

television	escalator	telex
calculator	computer	recorder
helicopter	X-ray	nuclear power

Musical instruments

trumpet	piano	xylophone
oboe	accordion	trombone
violin	recorder	clarinet
cornet	cello	viola
flute	piccolo	zither
guitar	harp	saxophone
harmonica	horn	glockenspiel

Dogs

Dalmatian	dachshund	Alsatian
Airedale	spaniel	greyhound
terrier	boxer	chihuahua
chow	Labrador	poodle

Cats

Persian	Siamese	Burmese
Manx	chinchilla	tortoise-shell

Stones (precious and semi-precious)

diamond	emerald	ruby
sapphire	agate	opal
pearl	garnet	cairngorm